ON A MISSION

Paramedic

By James Buckley Jr.

Mason Crest
450 Parkway Drive, Suite D
Broomall, PA 19008
www.masoncrest.com

Printed and bound in the United States of America.

Series ISBN: 978-1-4222-3391-7
Hardback ISBN: 978-1-4222-3398-6
EBook ISBN: 978-1-4222-8507-7

First printing
1 3 5 7 9 8 6 4 2

Produced by Shoreline Publishing Group LLC
Santa Barbara, California
Editorial Director: James Buckley Jr.
Designer: Bill Madrid
Production: Sandy Gordon
www.shorelinepublishing.com
Cover image: Dreamstime.com/Monkey Business Images

Library of Congress Cataloging-in-Publication Data
Buckley, James Jr., author.
        Paramedic / by James Buckley, Jr.
        pages cm. -- (On a mission!)
        Audience: Grades 9-12
        Includes bibliographical references and index.
ISBN 978-1-4222-3398-6 (hardback : alk. paper) -- ISBN (invalid) 978-1-4222-3391-7 (series : alk. paper)
-- ISBN 978-1-4222-8507-7 (ebook) 1. Emergency medical technicians--Juvenile literature. 2. Emergency
medicine--Juvenile literature. I. Title.
RC86.7.K45 2015
616.02'5--dc23
                              2015004835

Contents

Key Icons to Look For

Words to Understand: These words with their easy-to-understand definitions will increase the reader's understanding of the text, while building vocabulary skills.

Sidebars: This boxed material within the main text allows readers to build knowledge, gain insights, explore possibilities, and broaden their perspectives by weaving together additional information to provide realistic and holistic perspectives.

Research Projects: Readers are pointed toward areas of further inquiry connected to each chapter. Suggestions are provided for projects that encourage deeper research and analysis.

Text-Dependent Questions: These questions send the reader back to the text for more careful attention to the evidence presented here.

Series Glossary of Key Terms: This back-of-the-book glossary contains terminology used throughout this series. Words found here increase the reader's ability to read and comprehend higher-level books and articles in this field.

Emergency!

Paramedic Rich Davis never knows what emergency he'll face when he gets the call.

When Rich Davis, a paramedic in Santa Barbara, Calif., arrived at work that day in the fall, he didn't know he would save someone's life—but that's how it is every day for a paramedic. Rushing to the scene of medical emergencies, they are the first medical responders who help people deal with all sorts of injuries and illnesses. Paramedics are not doctors, but they are the people whose talent, compassion, and bravery make sure that injured people are taken to a hospital as quickly and as safely as possible. Being a paramedic demands focus and commitment. Then it's a matter of being there and doing the right things when the situation calls for a calm, professional approach. That's the way paramedics like Davis face events such as this one.

Davis and his partner Nick Armentrout got a radio call that a man had fallen on the sidewalk of a local college campus. Falls are actually one of the most common calls for medical first responders. In a single step, a person can go from walking calmly along to lying injured on the ground. A fall might seem pretty innocent, but, as happened in this case, it can lead to dangerous situations.

Words to Understand

airway the passage in the body that pushes air in and out of the lungs

cardiac having to do with the heart

lethal able to cause death

Davis parked his ambulance and grabbed one of the team's trauma bags, ready to patch up the injured man. His partner took along the team's **airway** bag just in case. As Davis crouched down to talk to the man, he called on his training to make sure the patient was calm.

"You have to be able to communicate with other people, you have to be able to talk to any-one," said Davis later. "You cannot be shy at all."

The paramedic quickly saw that the man was not seriously injured. Davis found only some minor scratches and a bump on the man's head. Davis and Armentrout also made sure the man did not hurt his neck. If they thought he had, they would have had to bring out a special piece of gear to keep his head from moving. However, when they saw that his neck and spine were not hurt, they moved on to other areas. As they looked, the man told Davis that he had felt faint just before he fell.

"He was an older man, so we put him on a **cardiac** monitor, just to be sure he had not had some sort of heart-related incident to cause his fall," said Davis. As a concerned crowd of people looked on, Davis put sticky pads on the man's chest. The pads connected to wires that would read his heart rhythms. The wires carried a measurement of the man's heart beat to the machine. As Davis watched the digital readout, his own heart got a chill.

Rich Davis came upon a scene like this one when he arrived at the college. A man was down...and needed help.

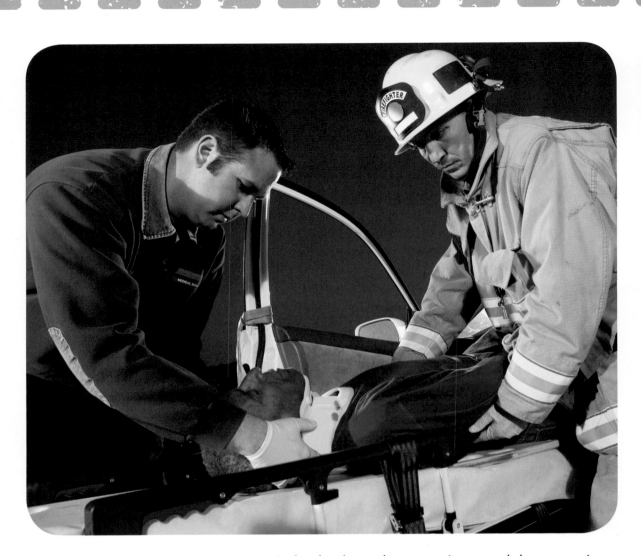

The first step at many emergencies is to stabilize the head and neck with a stiff collar to prevent further injury.

"I looked at the monitor and he was in a **lethal** cardiac rhythm. We realized that he could die at any second. I've only seen these a couple of times when the person had a pulse. Normally when you see that rhythm, the person either doesn't have a pulse or is unconscious. But this guy is sitting there, talking to us! He didn't know it until we told him, but he was having what we call a cardiac event. It's when your heart beats so fast that it doesn't have time to fill with blood again [after each beat]."

If Davis and Armentrout did not act immediately, the man could have a fatal heart attack at any minute.

Calling on his years of training, but adding a little creativity, Davis came up with a solution. In the next few minutes, his decisions and his actions would see that the man lived . . . or died.

Later, in the final chapter "Mission Accomplished," find out if Davis and Armentrout were able to save this victim. First, read about the training and gear that help paramedics save lives.

Chapter 1

Paramedics have to learn to be good communicators and listeners, along with being experts at medical techniques.

Mission Prep

When trouble strikes, people call 911 for help. The 911 operator listens and then sends the right experts for the job. When someone is ill or injured, the expert needed is a paramedic. Paramedics are important first responders. They use their medical training to save lives every day. It's a hard job, dealing with danger and possible death so often, but people who choose this for a career know that they are making a difference. They don't get as many headlines as firefighters or police officers, but paramedics are just as important and helpful.

Becoming a paramedic involves classroom work and practice in the field. There are important skills to learn and, yes, they have to take tests! Most paramedic training courses don't need a college degree to start, so it can be an exciting, important job, even for someone who doesn't want to go to college.

Words to Understand

cardio-pulmonary resuscitation known as CPR, this is a technique for keeping a person's heart and lungs working until help can arrive

psychologists doctors who help people with mental health issues

Do You Have What It Takes?

What kind of person becomes a para-medic? If you want a quiet job with little action, then this is not the job for you. Paramedics face new challenges every day, and it takes a special kind of person to be ready for that. They need to be physically fit as well, both to lift and carry patients, but some-times to make their way to wherever the patients are. Paramedics have to remain calm in very stressful situa-tions as well. They need to be great at working with a team, such as other paramedics, nurses, and doctors. Fi-nally, they have to understand that sometimes all they do is not enough. It never feels good to have someone you're helping die, but paramedics have to come back the next day and keep trying. "People perceive us as strong or brave, but I don't know if I'm stronger or braver than the next guy," says paramedic Rich Davis.

EMT vs. Paramedic

There are two basic kinds of medical rescue experts. The first is an emer-gency medical technician (EMT). After EMTs finish their training, they can help patients in the field, but they are limit-ed in what they can do. EMTs certainly can do CPR. That stands for **cardio-pulmonary resuscitation**—when a person's heart has stopped or they are having trouble breathing, CPR can help their heart keep beating until they can reach a hospital. EMTs can provide oxy-gen or give inhaler treatment to those with asthma. They take blood pressure and other vital signs. EMTs also ban-dage or splint wounds or broken limbs.

The second type of medical rescue expert is the paramedic. All paramedics have gone through EMT training, but paramedics take fur-ther courses that add to their skill set.

A fully trained paramedic is like an emergency room on wheels. They can give shots of medicine, start IVs (tubes that provide medicine and other fluid), put in a breathing tube, and other advanced types of care.

One way to describe the difference between an EMT and a paramedic is that EMTs cannot break a person's skin. That is, they can't start IVs or give injections, while a paramedic can.

First Steps

Like most students looking at jobs with special skills, future EMTs and paramedics have to attend classes. After applying to a school or business that provides the classes, they hit the books! To become an EMT, you need about 150 hours of work in the classroom and another 10–20 hours learning in the field.

In the classes and coursework, EMTs learn basic life support. That teaches them how to make sure a patient is breathing and has a steady pulse. They learn how to dress wounds quickly to stop bleeding. They also learn how to handle or move an injured person to make sure that moving them doesn't make their injuries worse. Finally, they learn and practice how to place people safely and securely onto a stretcher (called a gurney) and deliver them to the hospital quickly. Other important topics include proper use of medicines, local laws about patient care, and driving instruction. Safely handling the ambulance is the first step to a successful rescue, after all!

EMTs learn in the classroom from experts, and they also read books and watch videos as additional lessons. To go on their missions, they have to prepare.

After they have passed the tests given at the end of their class time, they learn even more in the field. Riding in ambulances with expert paramedics, EMTs learn the important skill of working with the public. When an EMT arrives, the patient is often scared and in pain. A good EMT knows not only how to help calm down the person, but also to quickly assess the situation and make the right decisions. Learning those particular skills is an ongoing part of an EMT's life.

Paramedics have to attend all the same classes as an EMT and qualify for that position. Then they have to go to even more classes, perhaps more than 1,000 hours in all. They will then train for several months in the field, working alongside qualified paramedics. Because they need to use many more skills, they need this extra time to make sure they know them all. Paramedics also spend time in hospitals, learning how different departments work with patients. They might work in the emergency room, with babies, with **psychologists**, or with physical therapists.

After completing all their training, EMTs and paramedics must be licensed. That means that the state in which

Paramedics in training use special dummies that simulate human reactions. Here, this trainee is learning to provide oxygen.

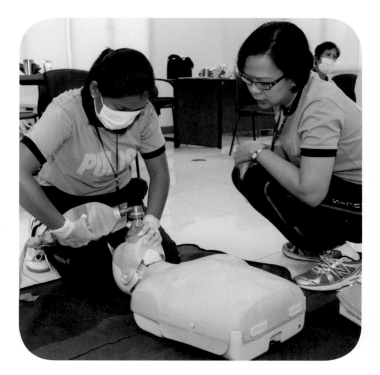

they live checks to make sure they are fully ready to go to work. Most states make EMTs and paramedics qualify every few years. They have to prove they are up-to-date on the latest methods and laws.

Getting the Job

With their license in hand, the newly created EMTs and paramedics can look for a job. Every state has different ways to hire people for this work. In general, though, a city or a county has paramedics as part of its fire department. Sometimes firefighters train to become paramedics as well. Other times, the paramedics ride alongside firefighters to emergencies. In some places, private companies provide emergency medical help, and paramedics can work for them, too.

After filling out an application and showing their knowledge and skills, some paramedics will be asked to make some trial runs. This gives the people doing the hiring a chance to see them in action and make sure they are a good fit for the job in that place. Some counties will also let EMTs volunteer for a while to both learn more and try out for the job. Experts say this is a great way to get a leg up on finding a job.

Right now, the need for EMTs and paramedics is growing. The U.S. Labor Department says that the number of jobs in this field will grow by more than 20 percent in the coming years. It takes time and hard work to become an EMT or a paramedic, but the people who do that work say it is all worth it!

Text-Dependent Questions

1. Who has to attend more classes, a paramedic or an EMT?
2. What parts of the body does CPR help?
3. Name two qualities a person wanting to be a paramedic should have.

Research Project

Find out how paramedics are hired in your area. How many work in your city, town, or county? Locate the nearest fire station or EMT station on a map.

Chapter 2

Paramedics learn bandaging and wound care as part of their training, often getting help from veteran paramedics.

Training Mind and Body

Training in the classroom is the first step to becoming a paramedic. All the books in the world, however, can't really prepare a person for what he or she will find when that next call for an ambulance comes in. Beginning paramedics have to work side by side with veterans to soak up all the experience they can. Along with learning all the body parts and the techniques of rescue, a paramedic has to learn about himself or herself.

The Right Mindset

Choosing a career as a paramedic means taking on a great responsibility. You need to make sure that you are mentally ready to deal with seeing some pretty awful things. You also need the confidence that your

Words to Understand

diabetes a disease that affects how a body absorbs and uses glucose (sugar), which can lead to other health problems with circulation and nerves

labor in this case, the process a female body goes through to give birth

training and your skill will be able to help the situation.

"You need to be ready for hard stuff, but you're never ready for it until the first time," said Rich Davis. "You need to understand what it is, and why it's happening, and then it becomes not as big a deal. I think of the human body as a model I'm working on. That helps me handle that."

Along with learning to handle tough experiences, paramedics might have to deal with some emotional pain. Sometimes, the call for their services comes too late or the person is just too injured, sick, or old to save. Then the paramedic has to be the one to give the bad news.

"You don't ever get used to telling someone their relative is dead," said Davis. "That never gets easy. It's hard every time."

Surprisingly, some paramedics have also come under attack by people even as they are trying to help. Some of the attacks are by gangs or criminals, while others come from people under the influence of drugs or alcohol. Paramedic Kristen Winters, who worked near Chicago, wrote on the FireLink Web site about a time that she and her partner were surrounded by gang members when she arrived to try to help someone they had injured. She was safe after firefighters arrived to help, but it was a scary situation for a while. When

Paramedics working in dangerous situations might need police protection or might even wear body armor.

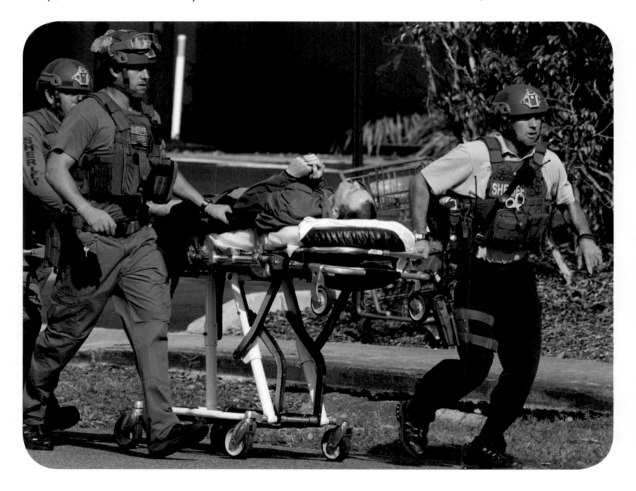

the police are not around, paramedics have to be cautious in such situations, adding another layer to their mental stress.

Fitness First

Along with mental fitness, a paramedic needs physical fitness. It is a job that demands strength and hard work. You are on the go all the time, and you might have to lift heavy patient loads. Sometimes just reaching the scene of an accident might mean climbing or making a long trek.

"It is a physical job. You need to be strong for sure," added Davis. "There are a lot of paramedics who miss time with injuries."

Paramedics make sure to work out and eat right so that they are ready to deal with the physical stresses of the job.

In 2012, the National Association of Emergency Medical Technicians reported a national rise in cases of very, very heavy people. America's growing obesity problem was causing problems for paramedics, who had been forced to carry heavier and heavier people. Paramedics sometimes have to build ramps or call in extra gear or personnel to help. It's not just in the United States, either. In England in 2014, paramedics had to use a special lifting crane to help a 420-pound (190-kg) man reach the ambulance.

Women are, in general, not as strong as men. However, this does not mean they cannot be paramedics. About 36 percent of American EMTs and paramedics are women.

"For sure, there are a lot of women who can do this job very, very well," said Davis. "In fact, I like having a woman as an ambulance partner. Her experience can make dealing with some situations easier."

Rachel Satterwhite was a paramedic in Ada County, Idaho. On its Web site, she wrote about

More than a third of EMTs and paramedics in the United States are women.

being a female paramedic. She agreed with what Davis said about a possible advantage to being a woman in this tough job. "I believe female paramedics may be able to connect with their patients more easily," she wrote. "On a regular basis I have the pleasure of working with a lot of strong, intelligent women. They stand their ground against guys twice their size and have the self-confidence to command a scene and direct patient care."

It's not the size of the person who is a paramedic, it's the size of their heart and inner strength.

Learning Never Stops

After people have finished paramedic training, they can take even more classes to learn special skills. They can train to transport patients in a helicopter or learn more advanced skills about heart health. There are special classes for paramedics to learn about how to care for very young babies, too.

Paramedics can also take refresher courses in new techniques or new medicines. Science is constantly coming up with new ways to help people and paramedics need to be up to date.

While most of the paramedics' calls deal with injuries or heart problems, there is a wide range of things they might have to deal with, and they undergo training to handle all sorts of medical and other emergencies. For instance, people with mental health problems need a different kind of help than someone with a physical injury. Paramedics are trained how to communicate with such people and assess their problems. People with **diabetes** also present special challenges, and paramedics need to learn to recognize their symptoms and deal quickly with what can become life-threatening problems.

Sometimes when women in **labor** cannot reach a hospital in time, a paramedic might help deliver the baby. Every year, hundreds of babies

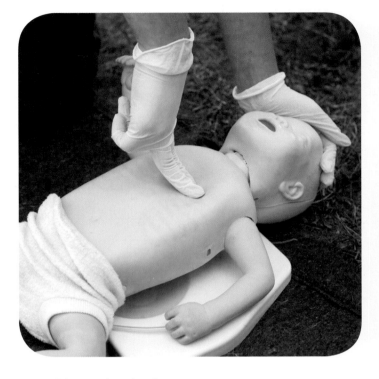

Caring for babies, such as performing CPR here, calls for special training. This baby dummy lets paramedics learn to handle their youngest patients.

are born safely in homes, cars, trains, and else-where thanks to the quick work of paramedics.

Paramedics have to work in all sorts of environments, including after natural disasters. When Hurricane Katrina hit New Orleans in 2005, Davis and paramedics from around the country rushed to help. Paramedics are on the site of forest fires to assist injured firefighters, and they are first responders when a bomb goes off or a building collapses.

"When I get to work at nine in the morning, I have no idea where I'm going to go for 12 hours," noted Davis.

Best and Worst

Paramedics train hard to do their jobs as well as they can. It's demanding work, but it does have its rewards. Davis said that the two best things about being a paramedic are:

1. Getting to make a difference in someone's life. "For me, I just want to make someone's life better when I leave them from when I met them."

2. His schedule. Like many paramedics, he is on call 24 hours a day for about 11 or 12 days a month. That packs a lot of action into fewer days, leaving him more time to spend with his son.

The worst things about this job are the lack of sleep when he is on the job, and often, he said, "you see the worst in people."

One more thing, though, makes his job one that he loves. "You get to drive the ambulance, and run the lights and sirens and drive fast. That's exciting for sure."

Text-Dependent Questions

1. What percentage of American EMTs and paramedics are women?
2. What is the hardest thing for a paramedic to do, according to Davis?
3. Name one thing that paramedics might learn from taking additional classes.

Research Project

Check your local newspaper or local-news Web site. Find three stories about how paramedics were called to the scene of an accident or a natural disaster. See if you can find out exactly what they did to help the victims.

Chapter 3

Like other paramedics, Davis has to be a quick and skilled driver, able to steer his ambulance through traffic at high speed.

Tools and Technology

Paramedics depend first on their skills and training. They have to be mentally ready to deal with any situation, from a house fire to a heart attack to a car wreck, but their training can only take them so far. They need the right gear to finish the job. Let's take a look at some of the important tools and techniques that paramedics use in the field to save lives.

Getting to the Trouble

The paramedics' list of tools starts with the vehicle they usually drive: the ambulance. These large vans are packed with gear, and are spacious enough to carry a patient in the back. The flashing lights and siren make sure that other drivers know to get out of the way as the paramedics speed to a call. The vans are heavy-duty, since they will be on the road for hours at a time and have to respond. An ambulance must

Words to Understand

defibrillator a machine that uses electricity to restore proper rhythm to a heart

extrication the process of carrying a patient from the field into the ambulance

stabilized in the medical world, this means that a patient's symptoms have been controlled or slowed enough for them to be taken safely to a hospital

trauma any physical injury to the body, usually involving bleeding

More Than Just the Ambulance

Paramedics have to use any means necessary to reach their patients.

Helicopter: Rescue helicopters carry paramedics into places that ambulances can't reach. These choppers are like flying ambulances, though. They have room for a patient on a gurney as well as for some of the life-saving gear the paramedics will use. In some cases, the paramedic might be lowered from the helicopter on a long rope to reach a patient.

Motorcycle: In crowded city streets, a big ambulance might be slowed down by traffic. In some places, paramedics zoom to help on motorcycles. They carry smaller packs of gear in cases, but can save crucial minutes reaching a patient.

Bicycle: At parades, outdoor festivals, or other large gatherings, a medic on a bike can often be the best way to get help to someone quickly.

be reliable, too; there's no time to wait for a new sparkplug when a person is dying. The paramedics are responsible for keeping their ambulance gassed up and reporting right away any problems with "the rig," as they sometimes call it.

In the front seat, the paramedic has a radio set to communicate with the 911 dispatcher and with his company or fire department. There is room for the passenger to work on paperwork while the driver steers. Personal items are kept up front as well.

Inside the back of the ambulance, along with the gurney where the patient is carried, paramedics have a stock of gear and medicine. Special cabinets, shelves, and racks hold medical gear, safety equipment, backup batteries, portable machines, and much more.

"The back of a typical ambulance is like a mini-emergency room," said paramedic Rich Davis. "We have more than two dozen medications and the gear needed to deliver those."

Along with medicine and supplies, all the following gear can be carried in a typical ambulance.

When paramedics arrive on a scene, most carry two basic field packs. One is called the **trauma** kit. This contains first-aid gear such as bandages, small splints, gauze or other pads to soak up blood or apply to wounds, and scissors to cut away clothing. There are wraps for sprains or strains and special pads to apply to burned skin.

The other pack is called the airway kit. The most important thing to assess upon arriving is whether the patient is breathing. If the patient is having difficulty, the solution might be in this kit. It contains an oxygen tank, a mask for the patient, and intubation gear. Intubation is a procedure in which a tube is put into a person's throat so that a special pump can help them breathe. Only paramedics, and not EMTs, can do an intubation—but it is often necessary to save a life.

AED: Defibrillators for All

The lifesaving tool known as a defibrillator has normally only been used by professionals. Now a simpler version is in use and it, too, has saved lives with the help of ordinary people. The automated electronic defibrillator (AED) is now often found in places where large crowds gather, such as arenas, stadiums, casinos, or train stations. Simple instructions guide a volunteer through the steps to shock a person's heart back into rhythm. It does not always work, but it has been successful dozens of times. Without the AED, those dozens—and more— might not have survived.

The paramedics also carry radios and other communications gear so they can alert the hospital that they are coming in. They can also communicate with doctors if they need any additional information to help the patient.

Reading the Heart

The heart is a person's most important internal organ. Paramedics often have to help people who are having heart problems. Their first move is to listen with a stethoscope, but they can also get information from a cardiac monitor. This device uses sticky pads connected to wires to give a detailed picture of the patient's heartbeats and rhythms. By reading the screen of this device, the paramedics get information on what steps to take. Their training combined with this technology can be life saving.

If the paramedics find that the patient is in grave danger or they have to try to restart a heart, they use another device called a **defibrillator**. The heart works on an electric rhythm, so this device uses electricity to jump-start the heart. Paramedics rub a special jelly on the patient's chest. Then they place a pair of paddles connected to wires. Pushing a button on the defibrillator, they send a jolt of electricity into the patient. It would

Paramedics can adjust the settings on the defibrillator to provide whatever level of electrical "jump-start" is needed for each patient's heart.

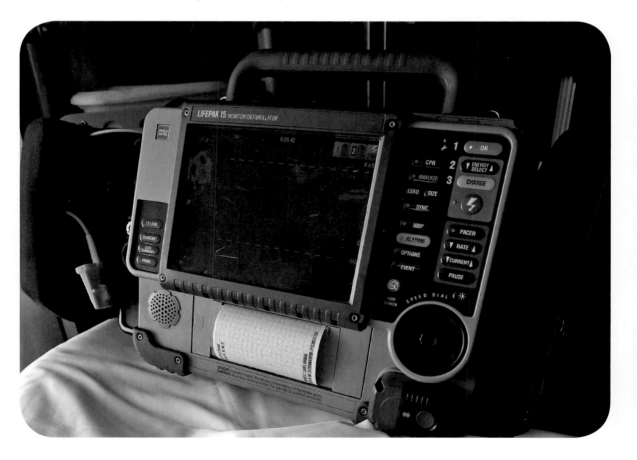

hurt if the patient were awake, but when a person needs defibrillation, they are nearly always unconscious. Only paramedics, and not EMTs, can use these devices.

Carrying Patients

After a patient is **stabilized**, or made comfortable and ready for transport, the paramedics use a variety of gear to move the people. The best known is the rolling stretcher called a gurney. These have a pad for the person to lie on, as well as straps to hold them in place. The wheels help the paramedics move the person from the accident site to the ambulance. The wheels and gurney legs then collapse as the gurney is pushed into the back of the ambulance.

Sometimes, a gurney won't fit into the place a person is located. Another way to move patients in that case, if it can be done safely, is the stair chair. This is a rolling chair with straps. The patient is placed in it and then the paramedics can guide or carry the chair down stairs or through tight spaces.

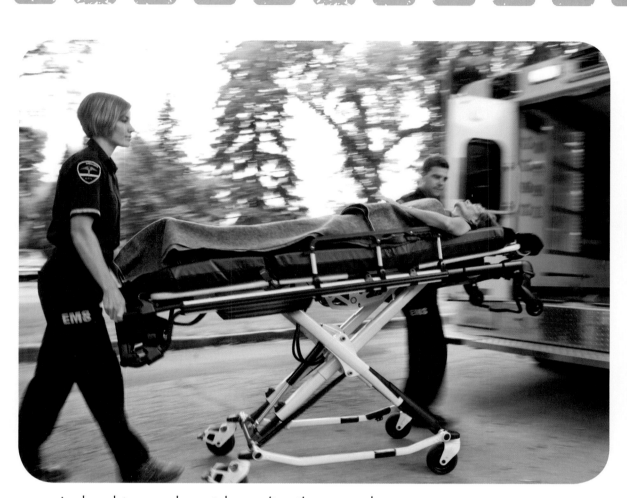

In hard-to-reach outdoor situations, such as on a hillside or far from a road, a carrying stretcher called a Stokes basket can be used. Often used by firefighters, the Stokes basket has numerous handholds and a lighter cage-like form, so that several people can grab it and maneuver it to a safe and level place.

The legs of the gurney will collapse automatically as the paramedics push it into the back of the ambulance. The gurney doubles as the patient's bed.

When a person has a possible neck or spine injury, an additional piece of gear is used to make them safe to transport.

"Any time there is a neck or mid-back injury, you need to keep that from moving," said Rich Davis. "The best way is on a flat board with a collar around their neck to limit the movements of their head. The board is great for **extrication**. We use it to help people who can't walk. We can use it in places we can't get the gurney into."

Staying Safe

Paramedics often have to go into hazardous situations, such as fires or collapsed buildings or even crime scenes. They carry safety gear for themselves for such situations. They might wear firefighter helmets, heavy rubber boots, and other protective gear to a fire, for example. Some paramedics are also trained as firefighters, so they will "gear up" in a complete fire-safety outfit before heading into the danger area to help a victim or a fellow firefighter.

Helping victims of crimes or police officers can sometimes place paramedics in dangerous situations. Usually the police won't let paramedics into an area until it is safe, but even so, sometimes a paramedic will don a bulletproof vest to enter an area to help someone.

From the smallest band-aid to the largest rescue helicopter, from high-tech machines to low-tech splints, paramedics have all the gear and tools they need to save lives.

Text-Dependent Questions

1. Name two things that paramedics use to carry people.
2. What does intubation help a person do?
3. Other than an ambulance, how can paramedics reach their patients?

Research Project

Does your family have a first-aid kit? Research the proper parts of a home first-aid kit and see what you have in the house. Then find out what you should add to make sure your home is prepared.

Chapter 4

Before bringing the defibrillator to his heart patient, Davis made sure the machine was ready to go.

Mission Accomplished!

On the sidewalk at the Santa Barbara college campus, paramedic Rich Davis faced a life-or-death situation. A man had fallen and, though he had no injuries, his heart was in a possibly fatal rhythm. Davis had to act fast.

First, the paramedics tried giving the man medicine that might calm his heart. As a trained paramedic and not just an EMT, Davis was qualified to inject the patient with the medicine. After a moment, however, they saw that it was not working.

Looking back on his training and his understanding of cardiac issues, Davis had to make a decision. This is where all his experience came into play, and where the calm professionalism of the paramedic took over. He had to try something he had never done before, but he felt it was the only way. He decided that he would have to use his team's defibrillator to shock the patient's heart back into proper rhythm.

Words to Understand

sedated provided medicine to make a person sleep

"Normally, when we use the defibrillator, the person is not awake," Davis explained. "As I prepared him, he asked me, 'Is this going to hurt?' I said, 'You will never feel pain like this.'"

As painful as that would be for the injured man, Davis knew this might be the man's only chance.

"I had never seen this, a person awake for the paddles, so I was kind of excited, too. But it had to be done because his heart could have stopped at any second," Davis said. "We **sedated** him with some medicine, and then we attached the sticky pads to his chest. The pads are connected to wires and the wires to the defibrillator itself. We calculated what amount of electricity we should used based on the readings we were getting.

"Then we activated the defibrillator. In other words, we shocked him . . . and it worked! His heart got back into proper rhythm. We were all high-fiving because no one had ever seen that before."

(Right) Davis, shown here with new partner Shawn Wilt, can relax. His fast work has saved a life. It's time to get ready to go back into action.

Whether they travel by ambulance, helicopter, bike, or on foot, paramedics know that they might be called on to save a life at any moment.

The paramedics quickly got the man into the ambulance and sped him to the hospital, where he soon recovered. Without Davis's quick action, the story might have ended very differently.

"Saving someone's life, that doesn't happen every day. We were on a natural high all day after that," added Davis with a smile.

It was a true "save" for the paramedics. They used years of training and experience, the latest medical technology, and a little creativity to come up with a solution—a lifesaving solution.

This is the kind of life-or-death moment that every paramedic might face when the radio crackles to life with another call.

"We never know what our next call will bring us," Davis said. "We just have to be ready for anything."

If you think you can be ready for anything, if you think you can respond with calm and focus in a scary situation, if you want to help others . . . then being a paramedic might be the mission for you.

Find Out More

Books

Canning, Peter. *Paramedic: On the Front Lines of Medicine.* New York: Ivy Books, 2009. —Note: This is an intense book with graphic scenes from the author's life as a Washington, D.C., paramedic.

DiPrima, Peter J. *McGraw-Hill's EMT-Paramedic, Second Edition.* New York: McGraw-Hill, 2011. This is a serious study guide for anyone looking to take an exam to become an EMT.

Mac, Carrie. *Pain & Wastings* (Orca Sounders). Victoria, B.C.: Orca Publishing, 2008. —Note: This is a novel about a teen who befriends a paramedic who helps him get his life straightened out.

Web Sites

www.emsmuseum.org/ This site has a great history of medical rescue experts. Check out the gallery of old ambulance pictures!

www.nremt.org/   The National Registry of EMTs is a good starting point for finding out how to take classes to become an EMT.

www.naemt.org/   The National Association of EMTs works with local and national leaders to make the work of EMTs and paramedics better and safer.

Series Glossary of Key Terms

apprehending capturing and arresting someone who has committed a crime

assassinate kill somebody, especially a political figure

assessment the act of gathering information and making a decision about a particular topic

contraband material that is illegal to possess

cryptography another word for writing in code

deployed put to use, usually in a military or law-enforcement operation

dispatcher a person who announces emergencies over police radio and helps organize the efforts of first responders

elite among the very best; part of a select group of successful experts

evacuated moved to a safe location, away from danger

federal related to the government of the United States, as opposed to the government of an individual state or city

forensic having to do with crime scene evidence

instinctive based on natural impulse and done without instruction

interrogate to question a person as part of an official investigation

Kevlar an extra-tough fabric used in bulletproof vests

search-and-rescue the work of finding survivors after a disaster occurs, or the team that does this work

stabilize make steady or secure; also, in medicine, make a person safe to transport

surveillance the act of watching another person or a place, usually from a hidden location

trauma any physical injury to the body, usually involving bleeding

visa travel permit issued by a government to a citizen for a specific trip

warrant official document that allows the police to do something, such as arrest a person

Index

Photo Credits

About the Author

James Buckley Jr. has written more than 100 books for young readers on a wide range of topics, including sports, history, science, nature, animals, biographies, and much more. He would like to thank Rich Davis, a Santa Barbara, California, paramedic, for his assistance in creating this book.